Reiki Hands
by
Jan Brown

Published March 2019 ©

Introduction

I have been asked many times for a book with pictures to remind students of the hand positions because not everyone finds a verbal description enough. For all of you who have asked, here is the book you have been waiting for.

Although Hawayo Takata didn't teach anything except where the organs, "glands "as she called them, were, she would have been familiar with the Chinese 5 elements and meridians which are used in the Japanese system of Shiatsu. Attaching chakras to the hand positions only occurred in the 1980's with the growth of the New Age movement. It never was part of Reiki.

For those of you who want some of the other correspondences to the body positions from metaphysical to chakras, then this is for you too.

As ever, if you want to practice under supervision, come to the Reiki shares which are held monthly. Details on the Diary Dates page of my website

https://www.reiki-in-east-sussex.co.uk

and on Facebook

https://www.facebook.com/eastsussexreiki

My grateful thanks to Wendy and Joanne who were the models for the photographs.

<u>Metaphysical aspects of a Reiki Treatment.</u>

Although I was taught the metaphysical aspects of a Reiki treatment, I no longer teach them in the class. I feel it detracts from the important aspects that you need to learn in class. However as there are times when it may be useful to know them, I have put them together in this book for you.

These are the hand positions for the head area.

1st position - **Over the eyes.** The hands are like two mitts with the thumbs close to the fingers. The heel of the hand is on the forehead, the palm is over the eyes and the fingertips rest on the cheekbones. The top of the thumb is between the eyebrows. The thumbs, being shorter than the fingers, allow a space for the nose. Please do not have the fingers too close to the nose or the person will feel they are suffocating. Please

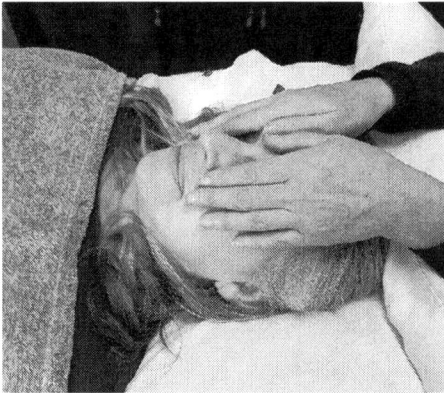

Position #1
The Eyes

Third Eye
Chakra

make sure you don't pinch the nose.

Eyes – Morals, values, decision making processes, beliefs and perceptions. The third eye affects intuition and Seasonal affective disorder (SAD). Sinuses – who

or what is up your nose or in your face on a daily basis.

The **Third Eye Chakra** has a colour of indigo and is all about intuition which can be in recognised in any of the senses. Some people are clairvoyant, some clairaudient etc. Good crystals for the third eye area are Lapis lazuli, Azurite, Sodalite.

Note the crown position (not shown) corresponds to the **Crown Chakra** and is generally a violet or white colour. Corresponding crystals are Clear Quartz and Amethyst.

2nd position - **Side of the head**. Slide the hands from the 1st position to just in front of the ears. Not everyone likes having his or her ears covered - I certainly don't. (This position can be split into 2 positions - Mr Spock (live long and prosper) round the ears and the lower jaw separately.)

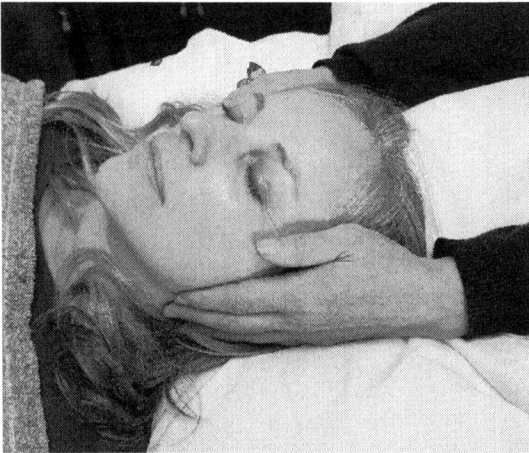

#2 Ears – Fears and phobias, cowardice and courage, helplessness and hopelessness.

3rd position - **Back of the head**. Roll the head gently to one side with the right hand and slide the right hand under the head. Roll the head gently onto the hand that is underneath and slip the left hand under the head. Both hands should be together cradling the head with the occipital (bump) in the palms and the fingers down on the top of the spine.

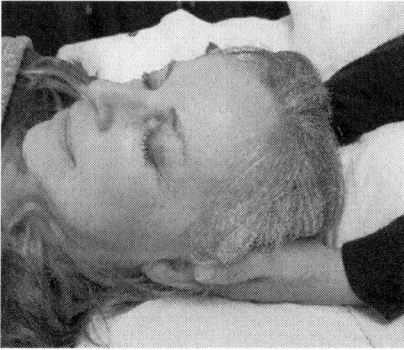

#3 Back of head – Past memories.

Cup hands as shown by the sculpture. You need to keep your elbows together to get that shape.

4th position - **Thymus and upper chest area**. The hands resting on the collarbone and the fingers tipped inwards to meet on the centre line (see 4b). This position can be split into **three sections**.

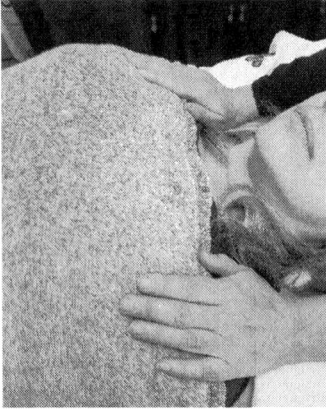

#4a Lungs – intake and acceptance of information.

4a Lungs Hands pointing straight down the body with

with the heel of the hand on the collarbone.

4b Thymus Tip the fingers inward from the previous position so that the finger tips touch in a V formation on the centre line of the body.

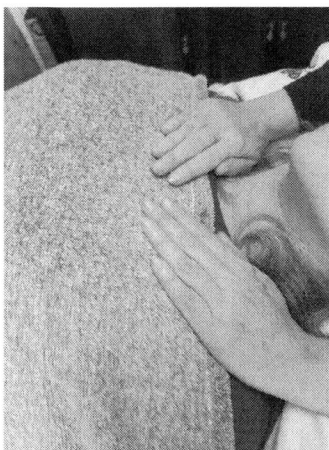

#4b Thymus— this is the main position.

Thymus area is the emotional immune system, psychic protection and seat of the soul.

This is the only position that is used in a 12-position treatment.

4c Throat Bring the hands slightly closer to the neck and tip them on edge so that you have your little fingers resting on the collar bone and the heel of the thumbs leaning on the jaw for balance. Be careful with this one to ensure that you are not resting on the throat or carotid artery, or the recipient will feel they are choking.

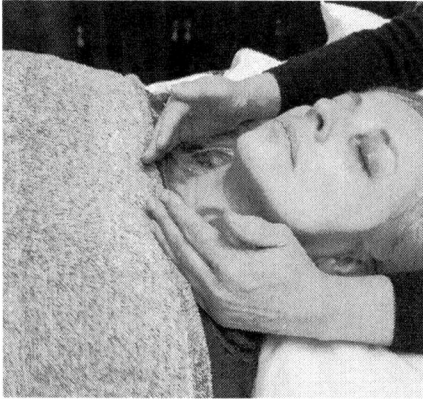

#4c Throat – Internal and external communication centre.

Throat Chakra—colour Blue or turquoise. Crystals— Turquoise, Larimar, Chrysocolla, Lapis Lazuli and Blue Lace Agate.

This is all about communications. If you can't speak out, or perhaps your internal feelings are

not congruent with what you are saying, this will show up in the throat area.

The front of the Torso.

Generally, the torso is treated from chest area to just above the hips. There are times when you may want to treat other areas like knees and ankles or feet.

Chest Positions.

5th position - Liver and gall bladder (and breast)

Move to the side of the body. The hands are side by side and placed just below the breast on the right side. (If the person has a very short torso, it is possible to place one hand above and one hand below the breast.) The hands mould themselves to the contours of the body.

The centre line of the body runs down from between the eyes, breasts, over the navel to between the legs. On the back, the centre line is the spine.

The hands on the torso always touch the centre line, this way no matter what size of body you are treating, you will reach the organs. In this position, the hands are either fingertips on the centre line or heel of the hand on the centre line. (It depends on which side you are standing.)

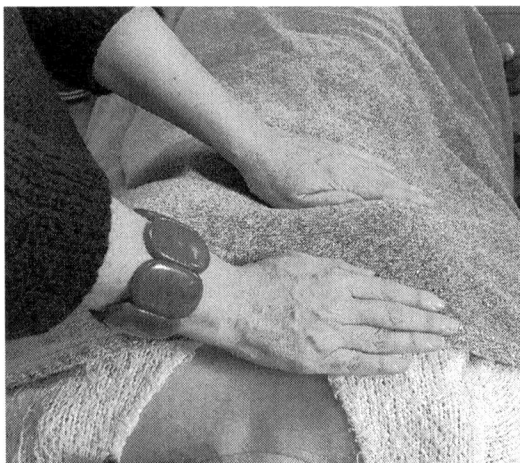

Upper hand covers lungs.

Breasts – self nurture, unconditional love.

Lower hand covers

#1 Liver – unexpressed emotions, anger and resentment. Also, memories of People.

Gall bladder – bitterness, peevish, spiteful, as in the meaning for gall and bile.

6th position - Spleen, pancreas and stomach (and breast).

6th position - Spleen, pancreas and stomach (and **breast).** This is the same as the previous position but on the opposite side of the body. Hands together with either the finger tips on the centre line or the heel of the hand on the centre line. The hands are below the breast (unless you are using one hand above and one hand below the breast).

This is a very important area of the torso as it covers all the major organs. If you have only a short time to treat someone, make sure you treat this area.

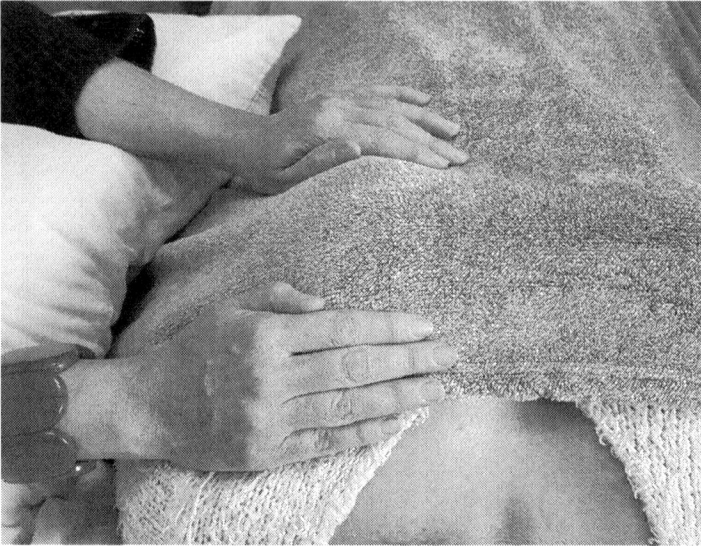

Upper hand is next Heart.

Heart Chakra is green or pink crystals – Aventurine, Jade, Malachite, Green Calcite, Rose Quartz, Rhodochrosite.

Lower hand covers

#2 Stomach, pancreas and spleen – again words or phrases associated with these

areas.

Stomach – acceptance or lack of (couldn't stomach/swallow that).

Pancreas – losses in life, especially those sweet to you – relationships, home etc.

Spleen – blood diseases as in hot blood, bad blood, angers and extremes of emotion, resentments and long held grudges, unresolved emotions.

7th position - **Across the waist.** This time the hands are one behind the other in a horizontal line across the body. The fingertips of one hand finish on the centre line and the heel of the other hand continues from there to the other side. This covers the small intestine and the transverse colon.

This is known as hands across—the waistline.
Always work to and from the centre line of the body.

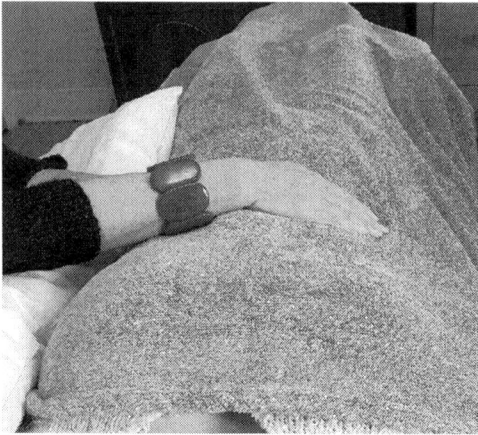

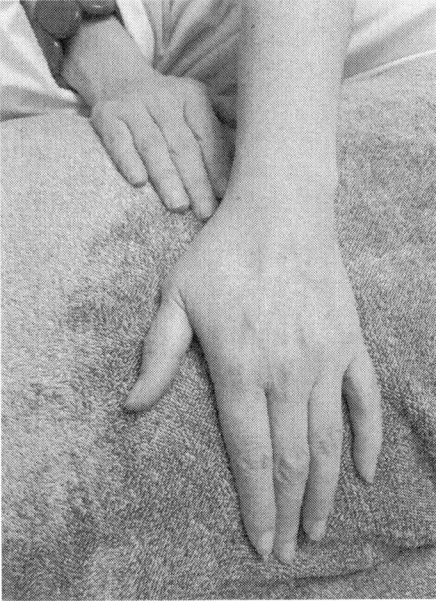

#3 Waist – intake and absorption of information. Useful for when studying for exams.

Memory - especially if you have forgotten what you went upstairs for. Put your hands on this area and you should remember what it was.

This area also covers the solar plexus chakra which is all about sense of self and unconditional healing. Also, to do with fear of failure which all about accepting yourself and not trying to live up to other people's expectations.

Solar Plexus Chakra has the colour Yellow. Crystals for this area are Citrine, Yellow Jasper, and Yellow Calcite.

8th position - **across the hips.** Keeping the hands in the same format, slide them down until they are resting just below the navel and over the hipbones. Don't go too low or the recipient will feel threatened. This covers the ascending and descending colon, the ovaries and uterus in women, and the bladder. For men, this covers the bladder and start of the prostate, which is treated from the back. However, if the hips require done, treat them down the side.

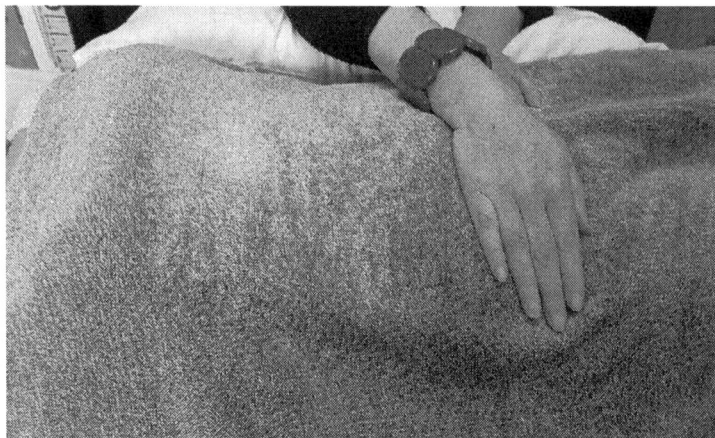

#4 Hips – Ki point or hara or dan tien. This is also the centre of gravity of the body and the splenic or sacral chakra and is all about self-esteem.

It covers the ovaries and uterus in women and the bladder area in both men and women.

The **Sacral Chakra** is orange in colour. Crystals for the Sacral Chakra are Carnelian and Fire Opal.

<u>Back positions.</u>

Turn the recipient over gently and make comfortable.
Again, you will be working to and from the centre line of
the body which this time is the spine.

There is a minimum of four hand positions down the
back. The idea is to use as many as are needed to cover
the back.

As Chakras are vortices that go through the body, the same correspondences and crystals apply.

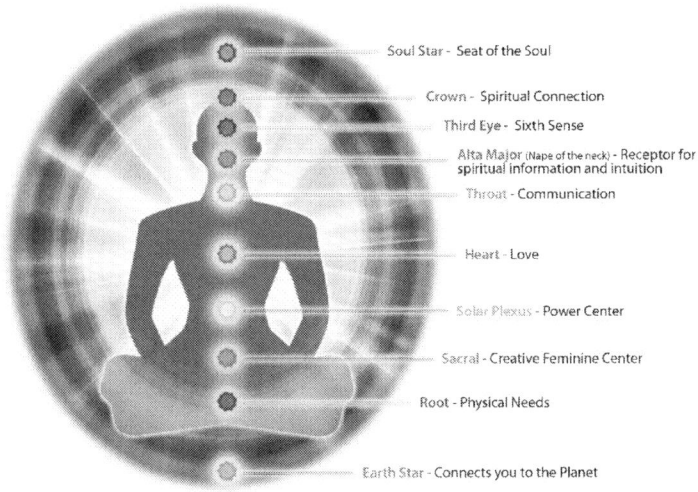

Soul Star - Seat of the Soul

Crown - Spiritual Connection

Third Eye - Sixth Sense

Alta Major (Nape of the neck) - Receptor for spiritual information and intuition

Throat - Communication

Heart - Love

Solar Plexus - Power Center

Sacral - Creative Feminine Center

Root - Physical Needs

Earth Star - Connects you to the Planet

9th position - **Shoulders** Hands for the next three positions are in the same format as the last two positions - across the body with the fingertips of one hand on the spine and the heel of the other from the spine. The hands are high up on the shoulders, just below the neck.

The top positions are all hands across and the 4th one hands together.

 # Shoulders – responsibilities and burdens, taken on and released from here.

This area is often really hot because we take on responsibilities that may not be ours. Learn to let go of those we no longer need.

Equally do take responsibility for your actions, good or bad. Let go of the blame game!

This is close to the **Throat Chakra**.

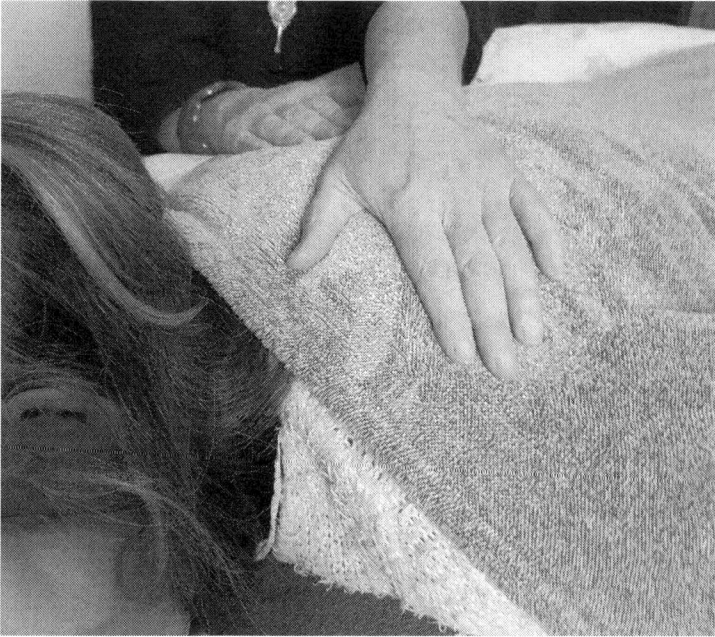

#Shoulders

10th position - **Adrenals.** Slide the hands down the back until they rest just below the shoulder blades. The adrenals sit on top of the kidneys (above the waist). In this position you are also covering the heart (and heart chakra) from the rear.

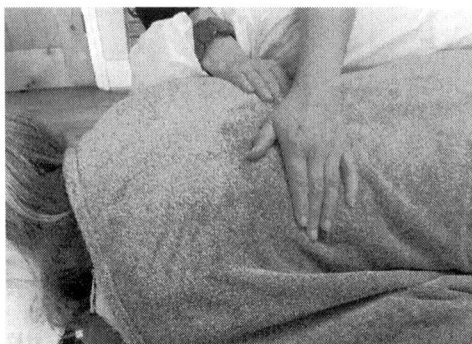

#2 – Adrenals – shock, trauma, extremes of emotion. Possibly addictions.

Hands across at bra strap level. Fingertips of one hand to the spine and heel of the hand from the spine. This is against the **Heart Chakra**, so the same colours and crystals apply.

11th position - Kidneys.

11th position - **Kidneys.** Slide the hands down to just above the waist. The easiest way I find is to slide down to the lowest dip in the body and then move back up towards the shoulders by about a hand's breadth.

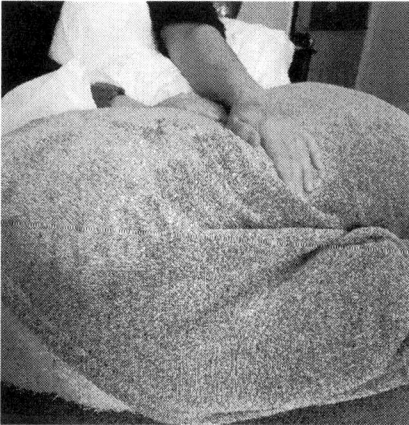

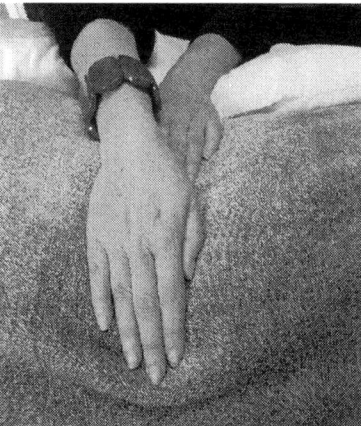

#3 – Kidneys – angers, resentments and being chronically "pissed off".

Hands are over the kidneys, just above the waistline.

This is also close to the **Solar Plexus Chakra**.

If the kidneys feel "crispy" then the person needs to drink more water.

12ᵗʰ position - **sacrum and coccyx.** Move the hands together side by side and place them on the lowest part of the back just above the cheeks of the bum. Treating one side then the other (cheek to cheek) if more energy is required can be done in this position.

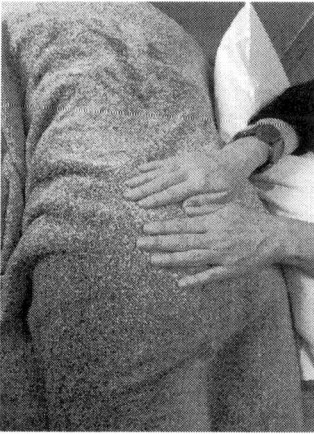

This also covers the lower **Sacral Chakra**. It may appear cold at first if there is a lot of trauma in this area. Treat for longer.

The "T" position is the one that covers the Base Chakra.

The **Base Chakra** is in the perineum area the bit you sit on—Its colour is dark red or black.

The crystals for this Chakra are Red Jasper,

Garnet, Ruby, Black Obsidian and Smokey
Quartz.

**It is all about survival and the basic instincts to survive
and live.**

The following pages have pictures of the self-
treatment hand positions. The same numbering
applies so you can see what the areas refer to.

Starting with the head

1st position - Hands over eyes with the palms over the eyes and fingertips on forehead.

Eyes

2nd position - Slide hands round to the side of the face in front of or covering the ears.

#2 Ears

3rd position - Hands behind the head as if lying on the beach. One hand is on the top of the neck and the other above on the bump of the skull (Occipital).

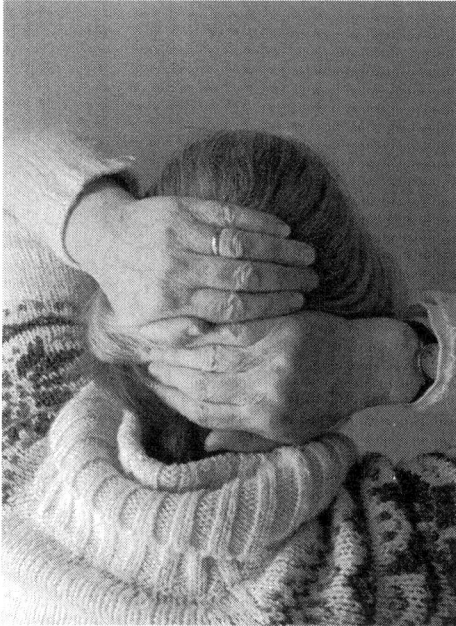

#3 Back of head

4th position - Hands over the thymus and lower throat. There are non-standard additional positions which I was taught but these are not necessary.

#4a Lungs

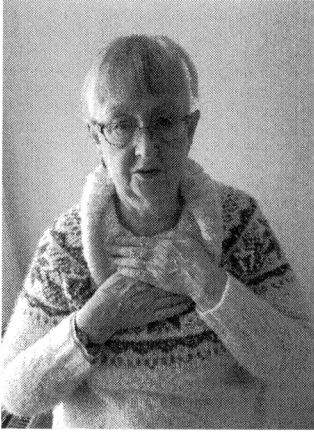

#4b Thymus

#4c Throat

Moving onto the front torso.

The following positions have the fingertips touching at the centre line of the body

5th position - Hands over breasts or if you prefer just under the collarbones.

#5 Breasts

6th position - Hands over liver and spleen.

6 Liver, spleen and stomach area

7th position - Hands over waistline.

#7 Waistline

8th position - Hands across hips just below navel.

#8 Hips

Moving onto the back positions

9th position - Hands on top of shoulders (one hand at a time if necessary)

#Shoulders

Or #Shoulders

10th position - Hands over adrenals (just above the kidneys) – difficult unless you are double jointed! You can do the positions separately.

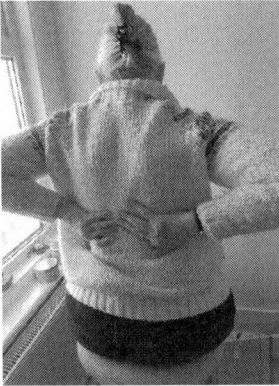

#Adrenals

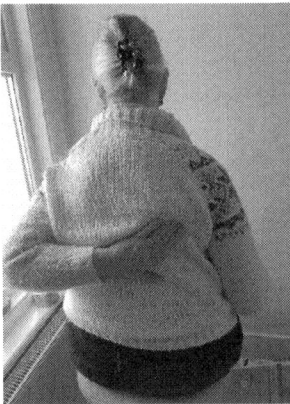 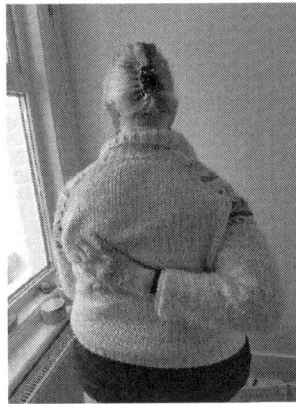

Or #Adrenals

11th position - Hands over kidneys (just above waist on back, fingertips on the spine)

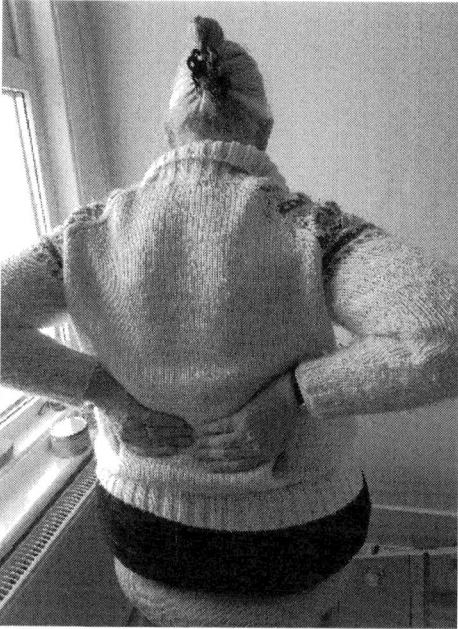

#Kidneys

12th position - Hands over sacrum with fingers pointing downwards.

#Sacrum and coccyx

Auxiliary positions -

If you have a long enough torso, treat **just above the breasts - good for repressed anger.**

Between the thighs is good for circulation.

Especially for men - sitting on the hands is good for the prostate.

Knees, hips, feet and hands or anywhere else that takes your fancy.
Knees – fear of death, fear of change.
Feet – moving on or feeling stuck.

Arms crossed with hands on shoulders is good for the lungs and helpful for sleep.

Throat – laryngitis and communication issues.

Note: In reflexology terms, hands and feet represent the entire body. Useful if you cannot give a full treatment.

I hope you enjoy this book and find it useful.

Please note it is copyright to Jan Brown. You can contact her on reikiscot@gmail.com

Janet can also be found on her website

www.reiki-in-east-sussex.co.uk

and on

https://www.facebook.com/eastsussexreiki/

https://www.instagram.com/reikisussexandkent/

https://www.pinterest.co.uk/greendigits/

Printed in Poland
by Amazon Fulfillment
Poland Sp. z o.o., Wrocław